Explore the Continents

Where on Earth are Deserts?

Bobbie Kalman

Crabtree Publishing Company
www.crabtreebooks.com

Explore the Continents

Created by Bobbie Kalman

For Erna and Dave Antaya,
who add much fun to our lovely town

Author and Editor-in-Chief
Bobbie Kalman

Editor
Kathy Middleton

Proofreader
Crystal Sikkens

Photo research
Bobbie Kalman

Design
Bobbie Kalman
Katherine Berti
Samantha Crabtree

Prepress technician
Katherine Berti

Print and production coordinator
Margaret Amy Salter

Illustrations
Barbara Bedell: pages 28 (bottom), 31 (whale)
Katherine Berti: page 30 (top left)
Vanessa Parson-Robbs: page 31 (penguin)
Bonna Rouse: pages 25, 31 (seal)
Margaret Amy Salter: page 30 (top right)

Photographs
Dreamstime: page 19 (top right)
iStockphoto: page 9 (middle)
photoff/Shutterstock: page 13 (bottom)
Thinkstock: pages 5 (top), 8 (bottom), 16 (bottom), 18 (bottom right, bottom left), 18–19 (background), 24 (bottom)
Wikimedia Commons: TimVickers: page 15 (bottom right); Steven J. Weber: page 21 (top right-inset)
All other images by Shutterstock

Crabtree Publishing

crabtreebooks.com 800-387-7650

Published in Canada
Crabtree Publishing
616 Welland Avenue
St. Catharines, Ontario
L2M 5V6

Published in the United States
Crabtree Publishing
347 Fifth Avenue
Suite 1402-145
New York, NY 10016

Library and Archives Canada Cataloguing in Publication
Available at the Library and Archives Canada

Library of Congress Cataloging-in-Publication Data
Available at the Library of Congress

Hardcover 978-0-7787-0499-7
Paperback 978-0-7787-0503-1
Ebook (pdf) 978-1-4271-8224-1

Printed in Canada/102023/CPC20231030

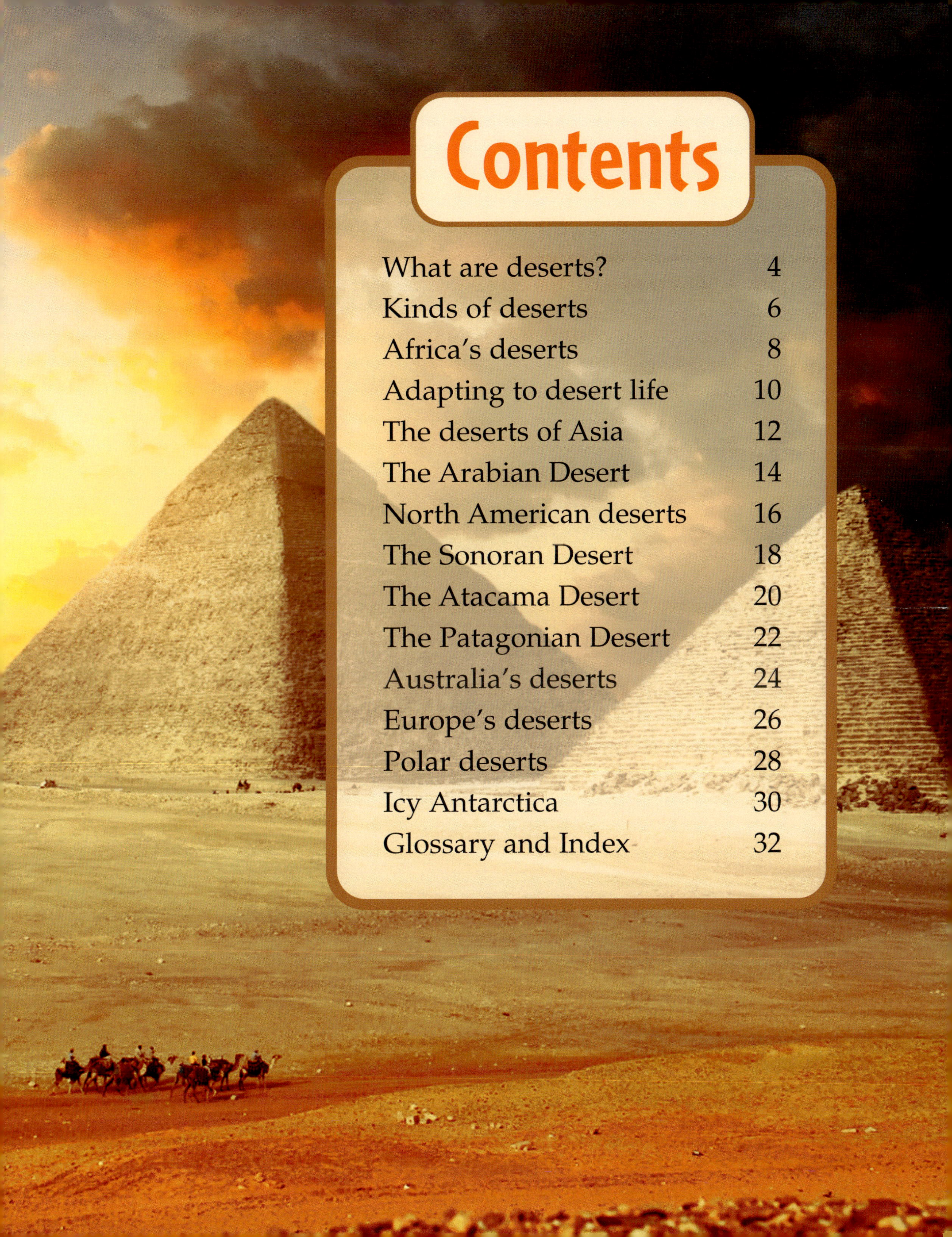

Contents

What are deserts?

Deserts are areas that get less than ten inches (25 cm) of **precipitation** a year. Precipitation is rain or snow. Deserts can be found on all of Earth's **continents**. The seven continents from largest to smallest are Asia, Africa, North America, South America, Antarctica, Europe, and Australia/Oceania. Find the continents and some of Earth's deserts on this map.

Some deserts are hot during the day and cold at night. Some get rain during certain times of the year. The Sonoran Desert in North America has two rainy seasons. Many plants grow in the Sonoran Desert. See pages 18–19 to learn more about this desert.

Kinds of deserts

The map on pages 4 and 5 shows you some of Earth's main deserts, but not all deserts are the same. There are **subtropical**, or hot deserts, semi-arid deserts, **coastal** deserts, which can be hot or cool, and cold deserts. Some cold deserts are near the North and South poles, where it is cold all year (see pages 28–31). Cold-winter deserts have very cold winters, but their summers are hot.

The Sahara Desert covers most of Northern Africa. It is a hot, dry, subtropical desert that receives only 3 inches (8 cm) of rain each year. Much of the Sahara Desert is covered in sand. ***Dunes*** *form when the wind pushes around piles of sand. The best way to travel on sand dunes is by camel.*

Semi-arid deserts get 10–16 inches (25–40 cm) of precipitation a year, mostly in winter. They have long, mostly dry summers. The Mojave Desert, shown here, is a semi-arid desert in North America. *To learn more about this desert, turn to pages 16–17.*

Africa's deserts

The Sahara Desert in Africa is a huge desert. It is the world's largest hot desert, where the temperatures can reach as high as 136°F (58°C). The Sahara stretches across nearly all of northern Africa. It covers several countries, including Egypt, Morocco, and Algeria. Two other deserts in Africa are the Kalahari Desert and the Namib Desert.

*An **oasis** is a place in a desert where there is water under the ground. The water comes up to the surface naturally or through wells. Farms, villages, and cities are built around large oases. The tall palms that grow in oases provide shade for people and for smaller plants.*

The heat of the desert can trick your eyes. Light from the sun's rays bends as it travels from warm air close to the ground to cooler air above. It can cause you to see a ***mirage****, or illusion, like a body of water that isn't really there.*

The Namib Desert is a hot coastal desert. It stretches for more than 1,200 miles (2,000 km) along the southern coast of the Atlantic Ocean in Africa. Very few people or animals live in this hot desert.

The Kalahari Desert is a ***semidesert,*** *or dry* ***savanna****. A savanna is a grassland with shrubs and a few trees. There are more plants in a savanna than in a desert, so more animals, such as lions and giraffes, can live there.*

Adapting to desert life

Both people and animals have to **adapt**, or adjust, to living in a desert, where it is hot during the day and cold at night. Today, many people travel across deserts by car, but some still travel by camel in groups called **caravans**. Caravans often ride for days without seeing plants or water.

People who live in deserts wear loose clothing to protect them from hot and cold temperatures. Men wear keffiyehs, *or cotton cloths, around their heads and carry heavy blankets to protect them in sand storms and keep them warm at night.*

Women wear long, loose robes similar to those worn by men.

The bodies of camels do not lose water as quickly as the bodies of animals that do not live in deserts. Camels can live eight days without drinking or eating.

Fennec foxes are the smallest foxes, but they have huge ears! Their ears help heat escape from their bodies, cooling them down. Big ears also allow them to hear ***prey*** *moving under the ground. Prey are the animals they hunt.*

Meerkats live in the Kalahari Desert. To keep cool, they live in large underground homes that have many openings.

The deserts of Asia

Asia has several large deserts, stretching across several countries. The Gobi Desert is the largest. It covers parts of northern and northwestern China and southern Mongolia. The Taklamakan Desert is China's largest desert. The Thar Desert runs along the border of India and Pakistan. Most deserts are dry and hot, but some deserts are dry and cold. The Gobi and Taklamakan are cold-winter deserts. The Thar and Arabian deserts are subtropical deserts.

There are few sand dunes in the Gobi Desert. Instead, there are huge rocky areas. Thornbushes and other shrubs grow at the foot of the mountains. Winters in the Gobi Desert are freezing cold!

*Many people who live in deserts follow a **nomadic** lifestyle. They move from place to place to graze their livestock, and they live in temporary homes. Mongolian nomads in the Gobi Desert live in round tentlike homes called **yurts**.*

Bactrian camels have two humps. They live in the Taklamakan and Gobi deserts in Asia. Their humps store fat. Fat gives their bodies energy on both very hot and very cold days.

The Thar Desert is a subtropical desert. Subtropical deserts are usually hot and dry, but the Thar Desert gets up to 20 inches (50 cm) of rain each year, from July to September.

The Arabian Desert

The Arabian Desert is located in Western Asia. It is one of the largest deserts on Earth. It occupies most of the Arabian **Peninsula**. A peninsula is a piece of land that is almost totally surrounded by water. Both the An-Nafud Desert and Rub′ al-Khali Desert are part of the Arabian Desert.

The Rub' al-Khali Desert is the largest "sand-only" desert in the world. Both this desert and the An-Nafud Desert are part of the Arabian Desert. Both are famous for their gigantic sand dunes. Some are more than 100 feet (30.5 m) high.

A few shrubs and trees grow in parts of the Arabian Desert. Gazelles, sand cats, and spiny-tailed lizards live there.

North American deserts

North America has four major deserts: the Great Basin, the Mojave, the Chihuahuan, and the Sonoran. The Great Basin Desert is the largest desert in North America. It is located in the western United States. The second-largest is the Chihuahuan Desert. Most of it is in Mexico, but part of it is in the U.S. states of New Mexico, Texas, and parts of Arizona. The Mojave Desert is the smallest North American desert. It is in the United States between the Great Basin and the Sonoran Desert.

The Great Basin Desert is a cold-winter desert. It gets about 7–12 inches (17.5 to 30 cm) of precipitation a year. In winter, it is mainly snow.

The mountains in this picture are in Death Valley, part of the Mojave Desert. They were formed from ***sediments*** *in a lake that dried up long ago. Many people visit the Death Valley National Park each year to see the spectacular mountains and* ***rock formations****. Rock formations are rocks that have been* ***eroded****, or worn down, into certain shapes.*

The Rio Grande River flows through Big Bend National Park in the Chihuahuan Desert. It acts as a border between the United States and Mexico.

The Sonoran Desert

All the deserts in North America, except the Sonoran Desert, have cold winters. The Sonoran Desert is the hottest North American desert but gets the most rain. It covers large parts of the southwestern United States in Arizona and California. There are more kinds of plants and animals in the Sonoran Desert than in any other desert. **Cacti** and **shrubs** are the most common plants. Some of the animals that live in the Sonoran Desert are shown here.

collared peccary

burrowing owls

jackrabbit

a roadrunner eating a lizard

kit fox

This coyote lives in the Sonoran Desert.

Shrubs are short woody plants. Cacti are plants with leaves that look and feel like sharp needles. They store water in their stems and grow flowers when it rains. In the spring, fruit grows on cacti. Some animals eat the fruits and flowers.

The Atacama Desert

The Atacama Desert is a large coastal desert in South America, on the coast of the Pacific Ocean. It is more than 600 miles (966 km) long. This desert is one of the driest and hottest on Earth. Some parts of it have not received rain for over 400 years! More than one million people live in the Atacama Desert. Some work in mining, some work in the fishing industry on the coast, and others are farmers who use water in the ground to grow crops. A few types of birds, lizards, and insects live in the Atacama desert, as well as gray foxes.

The Atacama Desert covers about one-third of the country of Chile. It is in the northern part of the country. The coastal area of southern Peru is also in the Atacama Desert. The Pacific Ocean lies to the west, and the Andes Mountains are to the east.

This desert oasis in the Atacama Desert in southern Peru is called Huacachina. It is a place where people go on vacation to experience a real oasis. The oasis has a large lagoon surrounded by huge sand dunes, on which people go sandboarding.

Gray foxes live in the Atacama Desert. They eat birds, eggs, fruit, lizards, rodents, seeds, and even scorpions.

The Patagonian Desert

The Patagonian Desert is the largest desert in South America and one of the largest deserts in the world. It is located mainly in Argentina, with a small part in Chile. The Andes Mountains lie to the west, and the Atlantic Ocean is to the east. The Patagonian Desert is a large cold-winter desert, with seven months of winter and five months of summer. Some animals that live in the Patagonian Desert are maras, burrowing owls, guanacos, pumas, gray foxes, and desert iguanas.

Desert iguanas are ***herbivores****, or animals that eat mainly plants. These reptiles eat the buds, fruits, flowers, and leaves of plants.*

A guanaco is related to the llama. It is one of the largest wild animal species found in South America.

Pumas are big cats. They are also known as cougars and mountain lions.

Patagonian maras are found only in Argentina. They are large ***rodents*** *that eat plants. Rodents have front teeth that never stop growing. Rats, mice, and squirrels are other kinds of rodents.*

Guanacos live in ***herds****, or groups, made up of females, their babies, and one male. Their only natural predators are pumas.*

Australia's deserts

Australia is the smallest continent on Earth. It is completely surrounded by water. It is part of a large area called Oceania. Oceania is made up of thousands of islands, including New Zealand and Tahiti.

The Outback

Deserts stretch across the middle of Australia in a large, dry area called the Outback. The largest desert is the Great Victoria Desert. It receives about 8 to 10 inches (20–25 cm) of rainfall a year. Australia's nine other deserts are shown on the map below.

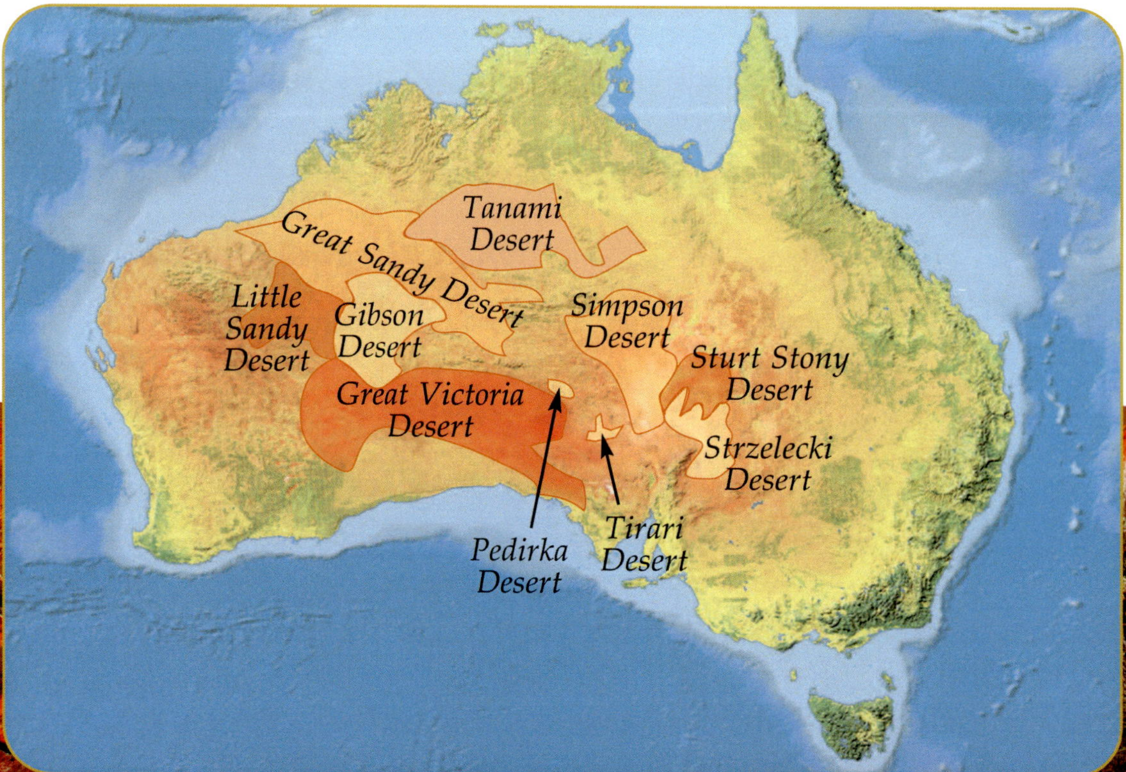

Many kinds of animals

Very few people live in Australia's hot deserts, but many kinds of animals can be found there, such as dingoes, red kangaroos, rabbits, and camels.

dingo

*red kangaroo with **joey**, or baby*

wild camel

*The Great Victoria Desert is covered with red sand. Grasses called **spinifex** grow in spiky clumps in this hot desert.*

Europe's deserts

Europe has a few semi-arid deserts, as well as cold polar deserts in the countries that are near the North Pole, such as Norway, Finland, Sweden, and parts of Russia. Some people feel that Europe's deserts are not natural deserts but are human-made. Europe's largest desert, for example, located in Romania, became a desert when many trees were cut down in the 1960s. People call this desert the Oltenian Sahara because its huge areas of sand remind them of the Sahara Desert in Africa. Other European deserts are the Accona, a semi-desert in Italy, and the Tabernas Desert in Spain, shown in the background picture.

The Accona Desert is a semi-arid area in Italy. This semi-desert has low rainfall, so few plants grow here. The Accona has white dome-shaped formations called biancane.

The northern parts of Europe and Asia are close to the North Pole. *Find out more about these cold, polar deserts on pages 28–29.*

The Tabernas Desert looks similar to the deserts found in the western parts of North America. Many movies are made in the Tabernas Desert at studios called Texas Hollywood, Mini Hollywood, and Western Leone. Above is the Texas Hollywood studio.

Polar deserts

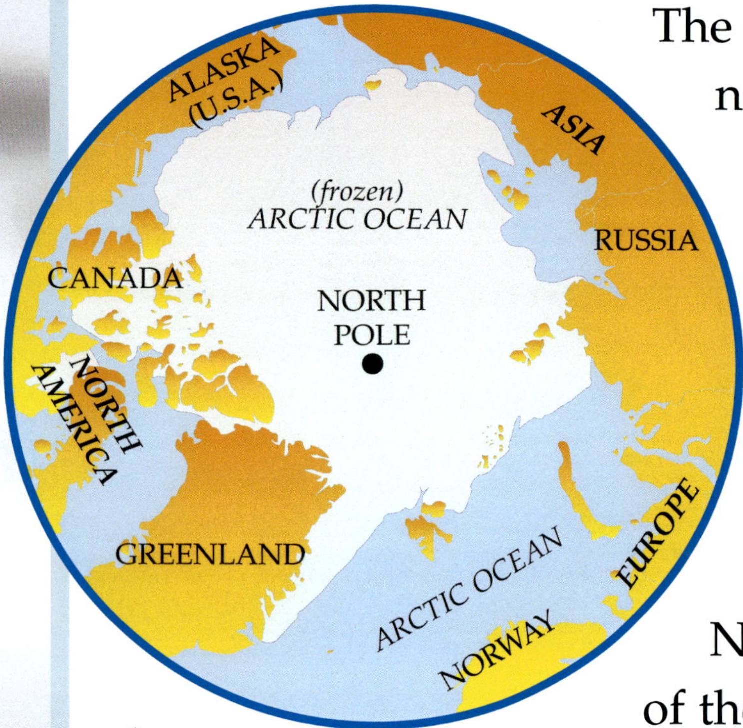

The North Pole is the most northern point on Earth. The most southern point is the South Pole. The weather is cold year round near the poles. The Arctic is the very cold, windy area located around the North Pole. It is made up of the Arctic Ocean, which is mostly ice, and the Arctic Circle, which includes the lands around the North Pole, shown on the globe above.

Tundra plants, like rhododendrons, have waxy leaves. Waxy leaves stop these plants from losing water.

The tundra

The land near the North Pole is called the **tundra**. The tundra is a cold desert that gets very little precipitation. Arctic tundras are located in the far north of the continents of Asia, North America, and Europe. Trees cannot grow in the tundra because the ground is permanently frozen.

Arctic animals

Animals that live in the Arctic have adapted to the cold winters. Some have thick layers of fat called **blubber**, some have thick fur coats, and some have both. Other animals **hibernate**, or go into a deep sleep during winter.

Polar bears live in the Arctic. They live in the ocean and on the tundra.

Animals such as arctic foxes, arctic wolves, and snowy owls change color in winter to blend in with the snow. Arctic foxes and wolves have two layers of fur to keep them warm. This animal is an arctic fox.

Icy Antarctica

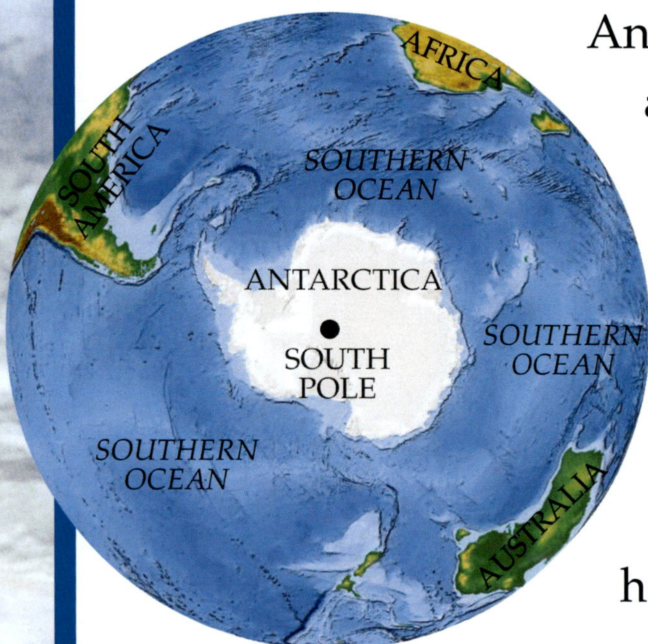

Antarctica is the coldest, driest, and windiest continent. It is a cold desert. Its climate is cold all year because this continent is at the South Pole, far from the warmest part of the world at the **equator**. Antarctica has two main seasons. It has a very long winter and a very short summer. Most of Antarctica gets almost no rain, and each year, a little snow falls. All year long, freezing winds blow across the continent. The winds blow the snow into the air. The blowing snow creates storms called **blizzards**.

orca

emperor penguins

Almost all of Antarctica is covered in a thick sheet of ice. ***Icebergs*** *are huge pieces of ice that extend above and below the ocean. The ice formations behind these penguins are icebergs.*

Adélie penguins

Antarctic animals

Most animals cannot live in Antarctica, but penguins can. Instead of flying, penguins use their wings to swim. Other animals that live in Antarctica, or spend part of the year there, are whales, seals, and many kinds of fish and birds.

rockhopper penguin

Antarctic fur seal

humpback whale

Glossary

Note: Some boldfaced words are defined where they appear in the book.

coastal Relating to or near a coast. A coast is land beside an ocean.

continent One of the seven huge areas of land on Earth

equator An imaginary line around the center of Earth, where it is hot all year

mirage An illusion of something that is seen but is not really there

nomadic Describing a lifestyle of people who move from place to place without having a permanent home

oasis An area in a desert where there is water under the ground, which allows plants to grow

peninsula An area of land that has water around three of its sides

precipitation Water that falls from clouds, such as rain or snow

sediment Pieces of soil, sand, or rock carried and left by water, ice, or wind

shrub A small woody plant

tundra A cold, dry, treeless area in the Arctic, which has permanently frozen ground underneath the soil

Index